ARTHRITIS AND EXERCISE:

A USER'S GUIDE TO FITNESS AND INDEPENDENCE

GWEN ELLERT, R.N., B.S.N.

Illustrated by Dave Hancock

THE
ARTHRITIS
SOCIETY

Canadian Cataloguing in Publication Data

Ellert, Gwen, 1952-
    Arthritis and exercise

        ISBN 0-9692210-0-2
        1. Arthritis - Patients - Rehabilitation.
        2. Exercise therapy. I. Title.
        RC933.E44 1985   616.7'22062   C85-091559-7

Printed in Canada by Hignell Printing Limited, Winnipeg

First Edition: December 1985
Second Edition: August 1986

Published in Canada by:

Trelle Enterprises Inc.
305 - 1775 W. 10 Ave.
Vancouver, B.C. V6J 2A4

Typeset by Elefont Graphics

This book is dedicated
to my parents
Lew and Bernice Ellert

I would like to thank my treatment team:
Dr. Howard B. Stein, Rheumatologist
Gillian Parker, Physiotherapist
Jackie Henwood, Occupational Therapist
Dr. Robert W. McGraw, Orthopedic Surgeon

Acknowledgements

For Medical Review: At the Arthritis Society, B.C. Division - Dr. B.E. Koehler, Medical Director; Bonnie Denford, M.Ed., Director of Physiotherapy; the Educational Team: Catherine Busby, B.Sc. (O.T.), Occupational Therapist; Bruce Clarke, R.P.T., Physiotherapist; Kathryn Duke, RN, BA; as well as Pamela Pethick, RN, BSN; Dr. H.B. Stein, Rheumatologist; Dr. R.W. McGraw, Orthopedic Surgeon; Dr. S. Hemming, Medical Health Officer, and Dr. F. Hemming, Aviation Medicine.

For Technical Review: Christine Allan, editor; Anna Daniels, B.Ed.; Lorraine Ewonus, B.Ed.; Gerald and Susan Pinton, Marketing and Public Relations Consultants; Michael Parker, VP, Vertigo Computer Imagery; George Ewonus, M Ed (Med. Ed.); William Preston, Executive Director, Arthritis Society, B.C. Division.

For Support: Thank you also to the many people who gave their input and support for the project and to my family and friends for their encouragement throughout this project and in the acute stages of the disease.

About the Consultant:

Gillian Parker is a Physiotherapist specializing in Arthritis since 1972. After heading the Arthritis Service at G.F. Strong Rehabilitation Centre in Vancouver, Canada for nine years, she joined the B.C. Arthritis Society working as the Education Physiotherapist from 1982 to 1985. She developed and provided education programmes for patients, peers and the general public.

Born in England, Gillian was raised in South Africa. She graduated as a Physiotherapist in 1964 from the University of Cape Town. Gillian immigrated to Canada in 1966. She retired from her position with the Arthritis Society in 1985 to raise a family. Presently Gillian maintains a keen interest and involvement in her professional specialty.

A special thank you for the time and talent donated by the following:

Production Team:

Ilka Abbott - whose experience as a librarian was invaluable;

Dave Hancock - who drew these special characters for the book as well as spending additional hours working on the technical format;

Michael Kluckner - author and artist, whose publishing experience made my life much easier;

Carole Vince - who patiently typed and retyped without even a sigh.

FOREWARD

The various forms of arthritis constitute the commonest reason for chronic disability. While prevention or cure for the more than one hundred different rheumatic diseases continues to elude us, virtually everyone with arthritis can expect improvement with a well-designed treatment programme. Arthritis treatment usually involves one or more of several modalities, including physician care, education, medication, exercise, joint protection, and surgery. This book focuses on the area of exercise where, in particular, it is incumbent on the individual with arthritis to become his own therapist.

The importance of strong muscles to give support to diseased joints cannot be over-emphasized, both in terms of function and pain relief. As the author rightly observes, the information in this volume should complement, not substitute for, assessment and advice of a physiotherapist. Exercising has all the excitement and appeal of brushing your teeth, but, like this important aspect of dental health, the arthritic patient's exercise programme should be an integral part of each day's activities.

I believe this book will provide an additional stimulus for the individual with arthritis to incorporate, into his daily activities, an exercise regimen.

Barry E. Koehler, M.D., F.R.C.P.(C), F.A.C.P.
Medical Director
The Arthritis Society, B.C. and Yukon Division

TABLE OF CONTENTS

Strengthening

Relaxing Exercises

Other Activities

INTRODUCTION

I wrote this book for people with arthritis, both young and old, and for the inactive who would like to *improve with caution* the flexibility and strength of their bodies. While the main focus is on Rheumatoid Arthritis the exercises are generally applicable for anyone with any form of arthritis. The book is designed to prevent the damage that can be caused by improper daily exercise, the wrong exercise or too much of any one exercise and will reinforce the importance of an exercise routine.

In this age of the beautiful body, "they" make exercise look so easy. Just put on your matching shorts, top and jogging shoes and head off to exercise class. But it is not as easy as it may look. In the morning I had trouble opening my eyes and getting out of bed on time! I tried setting the alarm clock half an hour early, but even the promise of "feeling better afterwards" was not enough motivation to make me get up.

I decided to try exercising at the end of my day when time was my own. But I was so glad to have made it through the day that I did not want to feel as if I had to do anything else!

For some reason I believed exercise must be easier for people without physical disability or pain to contend with. Not true! They may progress faster to optimum fitness, but they still have to have the willpower to get up that half an hour earlier and not to give in to the desire to "collapse" when they are finished their day's routine, be it at home or at work.

It is true, people with arthritis may be more fatigued. You may have the morning pain or stiffness. But it still is the "willpower" that counts: the willpower to do something *for yourself*, to take that initial step to becoming as fit as you can - however boring, however painful.

There is nothing I can do to give you the willpower to exercise. This book is for those who recognize the need for exercise, would like to exercise, but presently cannot keep up with the fast pace of exercise groups. We need a much more controlled and individualized method of stretching and strengthening our bodies.

There is no easy way to start to exercise. It will help, however, to know why you should exercise, and to realize that a person with arthritis has more to gain than someone already able to move easily and free of restrictions.

Exercise should be approached on a day-to-day basis. You should have a good understanding of what your minimum ability is and how you can build to your maximum ability. In order to build up to your maximum, a knowledge of the composition of a joint and the way it works with various muscles to produce motion will help you understand what each exercise is doing for you, and why.

Gwen Ellert

THE DISEASE PROCESS

Anatomy of a normal joint:

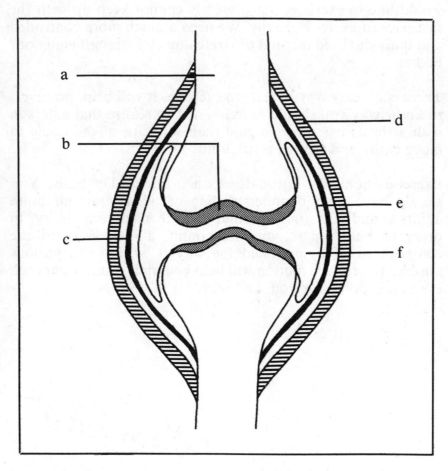

a = bone
b = articular cartilage
c = joint capsule

d = ligaments
e = synovial membrane
f = joint space containing
    synovial fluid

Bone

This gives shape to and supports the body. Offers protection to some organs (e.g. heart and lungs) and gives a point of attachment for the muscles.

Articular Cartilage

This covers the surface or ends of the bone at the joint, providing a smooth surface for ease of motion.

Joint Capsule and Ligaments

The capsule encloses the whole joint and, with the ligaments which reinforce and strengthen it, provides support to the joint.

Synovial Membrane

A thin layer of tissue which lies under the joint capsule and lines the synovial cavity. This membrane produces synovial fluid.

Synovial Fluid

A somewhat thick fluid which is produced by the synovial membrane and contains water and nutrients which lubricate and nourish the joints. The lubrication is necessary to reduce friction between the cartilage surface and the bone ends.

Joint Space
The space enclosed by the bones and the joint capsule.

The diagram on page 6 shows a normal joint. You may already know that the word arthritis simply means "joint inflammation". It is important to understand the difference between normal joint inflammation and inflammation caused by Rheumatoid Arthritis.

Normal Inflammatory Response:

Inflammation is the way the body reacts to anything that has invaded or injured the tissue. Normally when disease or injury affects a joint, inflammation also occurs in that joint.

The body directs *special fluids* to the affected area. These fluids contain cells and chemicals which help to destroy whatever caused the injury and to *repair* the damaged tissue.

With all this activity going on, the affected area becomes *swollen and hot*. (Hot because of the increased blood supply to the area; swollen because of the extra fluid in the affected area).

This normal inflammatory reaction uses up body energy. Therefore, you may find you are more tired than usual while the body is trying to repair itself. At this point it is a good idea to *rest* the injured area.

Rheumatic Inflammatory Response:

In Rheumatoid Arthritis the cause of the *inflammatory reaction* is not known. As with normal inflammation, the body responds by sending *special fluids* to the area. However, in the process of trying to heal the tissue, the *synovial membrane* begins to swell and thicken. It produces cells and chemicals which start to *destroy* the membrane, the cartilage and, eventually, the bone.

As the inflammation causes more *swelling*, the joint capsule and ligaments supporting the joint are being *stretched*.

At this stage of the disease, your joint is hot, swollen, *painful*. You do not want to move this sore joint. Therefore, after a short period of time, you will find the muscles around the affected joint become wasted and *weaker*. Now, instead of just one problem - arthritis - you have two problems, the second being muscle wasting!

This process does not necessarily create a downhill cycle. The disease tends to flare (become active) and then go into remission (become inactive). In a "flare-up" it is important to exercise properly and move your joint through the entire range of motion.

This helps to *maintain* the movement you have. Then, when the disease is in remission, you can *increase* your range and strength.

Ideally, you should exercise *every joint every day*, to some degree, especially when the disease is active.

Although it is essential to move all affected joints daily, it must be done according to the degree of heat, pain and swelling at that particular time. Excessive and improper motion may aggravate an inflamed joint.

Also, when the joint is hot and swollen the joint capsule is stretched. Over time this stretching could cause the surrounding tissue, capsule and ligaments to lose their ability to support the joint. Therefore, once you have exercised the joint, you should support it by using specific aids or "supports". These supports may help to ease the joint stress so that you are not stretching or straining the ligaments while they are vulnerable.

Finally, because medical science cannot eradicate the cause of the disease and cure it, the available treatments only help control the disease. It may take time to find the best treatment for you. Be patient. Work with your doctor and other members of the treatment team - such as the physiotherapist, nurse, occupational therapist or dietician - to find the treatment that is right for you.

The important thing is to get this treatment in the early stages of your disease - *before permanent damage* has occurred. In most cases the effects of the disease can be lessened by anti-inflammatory medication, rest and exercise as recommended by your treatment team.

REASONS FOR EXERCISE

By now if you cannot think of any good reasons for exercising, let me give you a hand:

1. The proper exercise for each joint will help to maintain or increase the range of motion, or *flexibility*, so you will be able to move more freely.

2. *Strong muscles* will take some of the pressure off joints that are damaged or painful, allowing you to move more efficiently and more comfortably.

3. Exercise will indirectly have a beneficial effect on your *weight*. If your disease is very active, you may have lost weight. Once the disease is under control, the weight may come back. This is good, but, with a less active lifestyle, you may find that over a long period of time you will end up carrying more weight around than you need - and that is hard on your joints.

4. Exercise will improve your *self image*. You will be doing something for yourself which will eventually make you feel stronger and more agile - opening up your world again.

THE APPROACH

Before exercising a joint you must know how far the disease process has progressed. Check each joint and *classify* it as either 1, 2, 3, 4, or 5, according to the chart on page 14.

Decide on which exercises you will do. Be realistic. You should not attempt to do everything all at once. *Always exercise the worst joints first.* A good way to start is to set aside 15 minutes twice a day. Some people find that doing the stretching exercises in the morning and the strengthening exercises in the evening works well.

If the disease is very active and you are not used to exercising, you may only be able to exercise your three worst joints in *15 minutes*. As you improve, you will be able to do more. If for any reason you miss a few days in a row, start back at a lower level.

Remember you are starting on a project for yourself that may take some months before it becomes a part of your lifestyle. You are the one who will benefit from the discipline needed to do your *daily* exercise. You may miss a day or two but do not let that cause you to give up your program.

Approach the exercises one day at a time. Remember every little bit helps. Do the exercises regularly. *Do not substitute* an activity for an exercise. Most daily activities do not use your full range of motion.

Listen to your body. Your guide to knowing whether or not you have exercised too much is pain. Two hours after having done your exercises, *joint pain* should be the same as or less than it was when you started. Increased pain means that you did too much. The next day *decrease* the number of repetitions.

Preparation for exercise:

You may find that you can increase your range of motion by first decreasing the pain as much as possible. Therefore, after you have assessed your joints, try one or all of the following:

- 20 minutes before you start to exercise take your pain medication.
- 10 minutes before you start to exercise apply an ice pack (or bag of frozen peas) to your hot and swollen joints.
- put on some music with a definite beat and rhythm to keep the pace going and take your mind off the discomfort.

The Skeleton:

Throughout the book you will see diagrams of an oddlooking skeleton with circles showing where the joints are (except for the spine).

The *red circles* on these diagrams indicate the joints you intend to stretch (primary joints). The *blue circles*, indicate any joints that may also move (secondary joints). You should be aware of, and cautious in, the movement of all the involved joints.

You may have *difficulty* exercising the primary joint if a secondary joint is inflamed. Try to find a comfortable *position* for the secondary joint. Start the exercise. If it is too painful then do the minimum number of repetitions and move on to the next exercise.

EXERCISES

This book will cover two sets of exercises.

The first set is stretching, designed to maintain and improve your *range of motion and flexibility*. Daily range of motion is essential for all ages and in all stages of your disease. These exercises will help to maintain the range that you already have. As the disease starts to come under control, they will help to increase your range.

The second set of exercises is strengthening, designed to maintain and improve your *muscle strength*. As your strength increases you will find that your energy level also increases. This increase in energy occurs as a result of strengthening your muscles. The muscles will take some of the stress of moving off your joints. Very soon you will find that you are moving more easily.

STRETCHING

Assess each joint and classify it as category 1, 2, 3, 4, or 5. Then repeat the following stretching exercises as indicated below. That is, if your elbow is a category 3: a joint that is a little swollen not hot and not painful, repeat each elbow exercise 5 times.

Category	Ellert-Parker Joint Classification System©	Repeat Exercise
1	Normal healthy joint, never been affected	10 times
2	A joint, at one time affected by arthritis, but which today is cool and neither swollen nor painful	10 times
3	A joint that is a little swollen, neither hot nor painful*	5 times
4	A joint that is swollen and hot or painful*	3 times
5	A joint which has been replaced (at present, this category does not apply to the neck, wrist or back)	5 times

*When doing your stretching exercises at these levels, push your joint just past the point of discomfort.

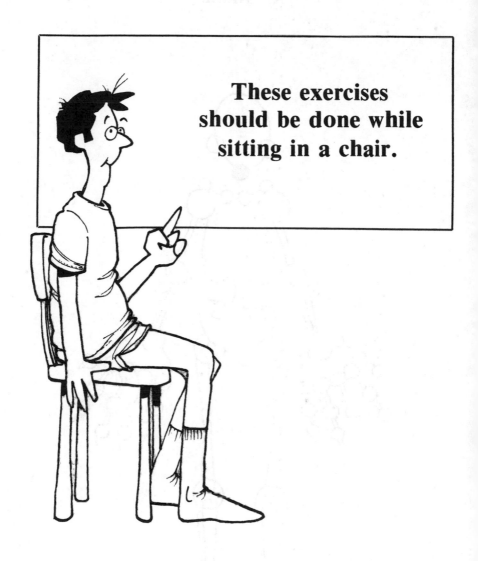

These exercises should be done while sitting in a chair.

I. Exercises "A" through "I" should be done while sitting
    in a straight backed chair with a firm seat and with no
    arms (i.e. a kitchen chair that does not swivel). Sit with
    your buttocks up against the back of the chair.

A. NECK

Some activities involving the neck:

- Almost any activity involves the neck: something as simple as having a conversation with a few friends, or watching television
- Driving, reading and sewing

Exercise Hints

- *When doing these exercises do not force your head down to the shoulder, or your chin over your shoulder.*
- *Just relax and slowly move your neck.*
- *When you are lying down and doing the neck exercises (page 62), your muscles will be more relaxed and you may be able to get a little extra range of motion.*

Lifestyle Tips

- When you are required to hold your head in one position for a long time, for example, when you are reading, watching TV, riding in a car, bus or airplane, remember to:
  - i. be aware of positioning. Hold your head in the neutral position, not bent forward, as this will cause undue stress on the neck and may result in pain across the back of the head.
  - ii. stop what you are doing and go through the neck movements every half an hour.
- Position of your neck at night is important. When lying on your side use one soft pillow that can be tucked well into your neck for support.
- Collars for neck problems are available, but *do not* buy one without advice from your doctor. It is very important that you have the right type of collar for your specific problem.
- Recurring headaches across the back of the head may be a warning of joint inflammation in the neck. If your neck is persistently painful, contact your doctor.

1.

2.

*

1. Look straight ahead. Drop your left ear to your left shoulder. Then . . .

   drop your right ear to your right shoulder and lift your head back up to the center.

2. Turn your head left so that you are looking over your left shoulder

   and turn it right to look over your right shoulder then back to the center.

*Caution:

Avoid putting your neck in either the flexed (chin to chest) or extended (tilting head back) position.

3.

3. Sit up straight, pull your shoulders back, tuck your chin in and imagine someone is pulling on a string which is attached to the top of your head.

B. SHOULDERS

Some activities involving the shoulder:

- Combing hair; putting on a coat
- Reaching for things (on a desk, in a cupboard)
- Holding a steering wheel when you are driving
- Tucking in your shirt

Exercise Hints

- *The "mid-range", that is when your elbow is straight and your hand is at shoulder level, causes the greatest stress on the shoulder joint. Therefore, if your shoulder is painful you may wish to put your hands together and/or bend your elbow while doing the exercise. It will decrease the stress and make the exercises a little easier to do.*
- *If your elbow is sore, first put your elbow in a comfortable position and then exercise your shoulder.*
- *If your shoulder is painful you may find that the lying down shoulder exercises, on page 64, may be easier.*

Lifestyle Tips

- When you put on a coat, shirt, or sweater, put your sore arm in the sleeve first.
- Adjust your cupboards and shelves, so that frequently used items are on the lower shelves.
- If you lie on your side at night, you may find it comfortable to tuck a small pillow up near the shoulder, under the arm on which you are not lying.

1.

2.

1. Sit with head facing forward. Lift your left shoulder up while keeping left arm by side.

   Drop your left shoulder down, lift your right shoulder up and drop it down.

2. Start with both arms straight down by your sides. Keep your palms towards your sides with thumbs up.

   Lift your arms forward and up to your ears. Then slowly bring them back to your side.

3.

4.

3. Put your hands behind your head and pull your elbows back. Then return your arms to your sides. Now put your hands behind your back and slide your thumbs up as high as you can.

4. Start with both arms straight down at your sides, palms facing down. Lift your arms out to the sides (as high as your shoulders). Then turn your palms up and lift your arms up to your ears.

   Now slowly return your arms to the height of your shoulders. Turn your palms down and bring your arms back to your sides.

C. ELBOW

Do each exercise first with your left elbow and then with your right elbow.

Some activities involving the elbow joint:

- Lifting heavy or bulky items
- Personal hygiene and grooming (shaving, brushing teeth)
- Eating
- Drawing, painting, gardening
- Answering the telephone
- Opening doors
- Using the gear shift in a car

Exercise Hints

- *Support your forearm with your other hand.*
- *Adjust your arm to get your elbow into your "comfort range".*

Lifestyle Tips

- If you drive, try to avoid using a gear shift car.
- If you must transport heavy things like groceries or suitcases use a buggy or cart with wheels.
- If you must lift a small child, have the child at your waist level (i.e. on a table or a couch) when you are standing. Then lift.

1.

2.

1. Start with your arm straight at your side. Bend your elbow, bring your hand up so your fingers can touch your shoulders. Then slowly lower your arm back to your side.

2. Start with your elbow bent at 90 degrees and tucked into your side. Turn your thumb towards the ceiling. Now roll your thumb to the outside (palm face up) as far as you can. Then roll your palm down so that it faces the floor. Finally roll your palm back to the starting position.

D. WRISTS

Do each exercise first with your left wrist and then with your right wrist.

Some activities involving the wrists:

- Personal hygiene
- Cooking and eating.
- Receiving change
- Writing or typing
- Opening a door with a key

Exercise Hints

- *Keep your fingers relaxed when doing these exercises.*
- *Holding your forearm still with the other hand may help you to get your wrist to its maximum range.*

Lifestyle Tips

- Never wring out a wet cloth but rather wrap the cloth around the tap and then twist the cloth with both hands.
- Use two hands for lifting pots and pans.
- Split the loads you have to carry into smaller bundles (e.g. carry one cup of coffee with two hands instead of one tray with four cups on it).
- For very painful wrists, custom made splints may help relieve stress and pain and therefore permanent damage. Contact your doctor or therapist for more information.

1.

2.

1. Have your elbow bent and tucked into your side, with your palm toward the floor. Bend from the wrist and point your fingers down to the floor. Then bend from the wrist and point your fingers up to the ceiling, pulling back as far as you can.

2. Keep your elbow tucked into your side and your hand out in front of you, fingers straight. Do not move your forearm (hold forearm still with other hand). With your hand, draw the largest circles you can in the air, first going one way then the other - (remember only your wrist should be moving).

E. HANDS

Do each exercise first with your left hand and then with your right hand.

Some activities involving the hands:
(very similar to the elbows and wrists)

- Grooming and eating (holding utensils)
- Doing up buttons/zippers
- Opening doors
- Writing or typing
- Handling money

Exercise Hints

- *Move and stretch each finger properly. Remember there are 15 joints in each hand.*
- *Fingers affected by the disease may want to shift away from the thumb. It is important to be aware of exercising your hands properly to prevent this drifting.*
- *Strong grip exercises, such as squeezing a ball, should be avoided.*

Lifestyle Tips

- Do not rest your chin on your hand, or push up on your knuckles to get up from a chair. These actions encourage the "drifting" (shifting away from the thumb) of your fingers.
- Pad or extend the handles of your utensils, pots, taps, keys, tools, car steering wheel, etc., so you will not need to grip the handles as tightly.
- A button hook may help you do up your buttons.
- A long ribbon pinned on to the end of a zipper will help when doing up a zipper.
- Choose a fatter pencil or pen when writing.
- Carry small, lighter loads - even if you must make more trips.
- Use two hands to pick up and carry heavy items.
- When shaking hands with a person, take his hand first and grip only his fingers.

1.

2.

3.

1. Gently tuck the tips of your fingers into their inside base. Keep your knuckles straight, make sure that they do not move. Then stretch them back out.

2. Start with your fingers together, then gently tuck them into the palm of your hand. Close your hand to make a loose fist. Then, slowly stretch your fingers back out straight.

3. Touch your thumb to the tip of each finger of your hand.

4.

5.

4. Stretch your thumb as far away from your fingers as possible and then relax.

5. Start with your hand flat on a surface, fingers straight. Slide thumb away from fingers. Then slide index finger toward thumb, long finger to index (keeping the rest of your hand still). Slide your ring finger to the long finger and baby finger over to ring finger. Then relax.

F. HIPS

Do each exercise first with your left leg and then with your right leg.

Some activities involving the hips:

- Getting in and out of a bathtub or a car
- Putting on your socks and shoes
- Walking and climbing stairs
- Sitting and bending

Exercise Hints

- *If you have a hip replacement you may wish to obtain the "Owner's Manual" (see booklist, page 121).*
- *For maximum benefit totally relax your leg muscles between each leg lift.*
- *Do not do these exercises too quickly. Be sure to stretch a little farther than you think you can.*

Lifestyle Tips

- A stick with a hook on the end of it will help you to avoid bending over to pick things up.
- Sit on firm high seats.
- At night you may find it helps to sleep with a pillow between your legs when lying on your side.
- Avoid climbing stairs if your hips are sore.
- Do not cross your knees if your hips are sore, as this puts unnecessary stress on the hips.
- If you need to push yourself up off a chair, push from your palms not your fingers. Be aware that you do not want to stress your fingers and cause them to drift.
- Avoid sitting for long periods. Walk or shift your position every half hour.

1.

1. Start with your hands resting on your lap and your back straight. Lift your knee to your chest as far as possible. Then . . .

. . . slowly lower your leg and put your foot back on the ground.

G. KNEES

Do each exercise first with the left leg and then with the right leg.

Some activities involving the knee joints:

- Getting up from a chair and sitting down
- Walking
- Climbing stairs

Exercise Hints

- *If you have a knee replacement you may wish to obtain the "Owner's Manual" (see booklist page 121).*
- *It is very easy to lose some range in your knee without even noticing it. You can cope very well with some degree of loss, but if the knee does not straighten fully the stress on the knee increases. It is very important to concentrate on straightening your knee.*

Lifestyle Tips

- Sit on firm, high seats.
- Avoid stairs when your knees are sore.
- Walking is good exercise for your heart and lungs but do not overdo it or push yourself. End the walk *before* you get tired so that you can do the walk the next day as well.
- Build up the seats that you sit on by:
  - i) using a solid cushion on a firm chair
  - ii) using a cushion when in your car
  - iii) raising the height of the seat of your toilet.
- When on your feet a lot, wear low heeled shoes with good support.
- Avoid standing still in any one spot for any length of time.
- Sit on a high stool while you wash dishes, prepare food or work at a work bench.

1.

1. Lift your foot up as high as your knee, keeping your toes pointed at the ceiling and your leg as straight as you can. Hold this position and try to straighten a little more.

Now bend your knee and pull your foot back as far as possible under your chair.

H. ANKLES

Do each exercise first with the left ankle and then with the right ankle.

Some activities involving the ankle joint:

- Walking, especially on uneven ground
- Driving a car
- Standing
- Climbing stairs

Exercise Hints

- *This is another joint in which you may not notice a loss of range. Therefore, concentrate when you are exercising in order to reach that maximum stretch. You will feel it across the front of your ankle when you point your toes and up the back of your leg when you pull your foot up.*

Lifestyle Hints

- Avoid standing still in any one spot for any length of time.
- Sit on a high stool while you wash dishes, prepare food or work at your work bench.
- Keep your feet up whenever possible.
- Wear good shoes with low heels, good arch supports and laces or velcro fasteners. Insoles may be helpful as well. Save your party shoes for a party where you can sit down.
- If you must go to a meeting or reception, find a chair so you do not stand all night.
- When you go for a walk, be sure you walk on even ground, not on rocks, sand or ground with potholes.

1.

2.

1. Point your toes down as far as possible (feel the pull on your ankle). Then, pull up and point your toes toward your head.

2. Draw a circle in the air with your big toe (be sure to keep your leg still and move only your ankle).

I. TOES

Do each exercise first with the left foot and then with the right foot.

Some activities involving the toe joints:

- Climbing stairs
- Balancing when you walk
- Prolonged standing

Exercise Hints

- *You can see from the diagram on the previous page that there are a number of joints in your foot. Be sure to exercise every one of them. A problem with any one joint can cause you to protect that foot. If you do not take proper care of that joint, eventually you may have trouble with the whole foot.*

Lifestyle Tips

- As with the ankles, your shoes are extremely important to your toes. Badly fitting shoes or insoles may do more harm than good. If you need to have a pair of custom made shoes or insoles, contact your nearest arthritis center for a recommendation of someone who can make shoes or insoles for arthritic feet.

- With any pair of shoes, be sure that you have adequate room for your toes.

1.

1. Start with your feet flat on the floor. Keep your toes straight as you lift your arch and slide the toes back toward the heel. Relax. Then stretch your toes apart as far as possible.

J. BACK

This is the section of the book where you would expect to find the back stretching exercises. These have not been forgotten, but on purpose have not been included as the back is a very special area.

There are some very basic trunk exercises on pages 102 to 107. But if you do have a back problem, then you will need advice from your doctor or therapist as to which exercises you should do for your particular problem.

**These exercises should be done
while lying on a bed
or the floor.**

II. Exercises "A" through "D" should be done while lying
on a bed or, if possible, lying on the floor.

A.   NECK

1.

2.

(Refer to pages 16 and 17 for joints that will move and exercise hints).

1. With your head as flat on the bed as possible, turn your head first to the left, then back to the center. Now turn to the right and back to the center.

2. Slide your left ear to your left shoulder, then slide your head back to the center. Now slide your right ear to your right shoulder and then slide your head back to the center.

B. SHOULDERS

Do each exercise first with your left shoulder/arm and then with your right shoulder/arm.

1.

2.

(Refer to pages 22 and 23 for joints that will move and exercise hints).

1. Start with your arms at your sides. Slide one arm out from the side and up to shoulder level.

    Keep your arm straight, turn your palm towards the ceiling and slide your arm up to touch your ear. Now slowly slide your arm back to your side.

2. Scoot down into the middle of the bed. Start with your arms at your sides. Now lead with your thumb and slowly raise your staight arm up above your head . . .

    lower your arm behind your head to touch the bed. Then slowly return your arm to your side.

3.

4.

5.

3. Bend your elbow 90 degrees and tuck it into your side. Slowly move your forearm as far away from your body as possible. Then . . .

    bring it back to your side and move the same forearm across your stomach and back to your side.

4. *DO THIS EXERCISE WITH CAUTION.*
    DO NOT put any pressure on the back of your neck. Put your hand behind your neck and lift your elbow up as high as your shoulder. Then . . .

    keeping your elbow at shoulder level, move your elbow behind your head and shoulder as far as possible. Feel the stretch and then slowly relax.

5. Lift your shoulder up as far as possible to your ear (do not bend your head down to your shoulder).

    Slowly lower your shoulder, feeling the pull down as you lower it.

C. HIPS

Lie on your back and do each exercise first with your left leg
and then with your right.

1.

2.

(Refer to pages 42 and 43 for joints that will move and exercise hints).

1. Start with both legs together and straight. Lead with your heel and keep toes pointed up to the ceiling.

    Slowly slide your leg out to the side then bring it back to the center.

    (Make sure that you are sliding your leg - do not lift your leg off the bed).

2. Bend one leg - keep the other straight. Using the leg that is straight, bend that ankle and point that foot to the ceiling. Slowly roll that foot out.

    Then bring your foot back up and point your toes to the ceiling. Now roll the foot in and then bring it back to point to the ceiling.

3.

3. Bend both knees. Lift your left knee up as close to your left shoulder as possible.

Now slowly lower your leg back so that your foot is back on the bed - your knee is still bent.

D. KNEES

Do each exercise first with your left leg and then with your right leg.

1.

2.

(Refer to pages 46 and 47 for joints that will move and exercise hints).

1. With the backs of your knees touching the bed, bend one knee, keeping your heel on the bed.

    Bring the heel as close to your buttocks as possible. Then slowly slide your heel back out so that your leg is straight.

2. With your leg straight, push the back of your knee into the bed.

    At the same time try to lift your heel up off the bed and point the big toe at your head.

STRENGTHENING

The key to strengthening the muscle surrounding an arthritic joint is repetitive movement, against gravity, with a "concentrated hold" to make that muscle work. With the stretching exercises you have been rhythmically moving through the range of motion, and then back to your starting position. Now, with the *strengthening exercises* you want to move your body part into the correct position, tighten the muscle and hold it tightly by concentrating on it for ten seconds. After ten seconds, you should completely relax the muscle and put your body part back into the starting position. You should do a "concentrated hold" on each muscle group at least three times. Put your body in a position that will be comfortable for you and do the best you can when you tighten that muscle.

STRENGTHENING

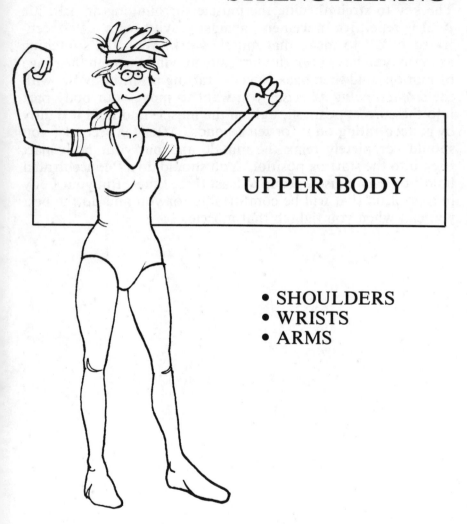

UPPER BODY

- SHOULDERS
- WRISTS
- ARMS

I. **UPPER BODY** - Shoulders and Arms (shoulder, elbow and wrist joints)

Refer to the joint category 1, 2, 3, 4, or 5 which you selected for each joint and repeat the following upper body strengthening exercises as indicated below. For example, if your shoulder is category 4 "a joint that is swollen and hot or painful" repeat each shoulder exercise 3 times.

Category	Ellert-Parker Joint Classification System©	Repeat Exercise
1	Normal healthy joint, never been affected	10 times
2	A joint, at one time affected by arthritis, but which today is cool and neither swollen nor painful	10 times
3	A joint that is a little swollen, neither hot nor painful	5 times
4	A joint that is swollen and hot or painful	3 times
5	A joint which has been replaced (at present this category does not apply to the neck, wrist or back)	5 times

A. SHOULDERS

Do each exercise first with your left shoulder and then with your right shoulder.

Exercise Hints

- *You may wish to place a small towel between your shoulder and the wall to add a little padding.*
- *Concentrate and feel the muscles around your shoulder as they tighten. If you are doing the exercise properly, you should be using only the shoulder and your upper arm muscles.*

Lifestyle Tips

- Extend the handles on your personal hygiene items (e.g. hairbrush, comb, toothbush, etc.).
- Most drug stores carry a back brush which will help you with washing your back.
- Buy clothes that open in the front instead of ones that button up the back or pull over your head.
- Use extended drinking straws.
- Use a dressing stick (a stick with a hook on the end) to help pull on your clothes or coat.
- A well-placed safety pin attached to a long ribbon will also help you pull on your clothes.
- A "reacher" - a stick with a curve like a cane - will help you reach for things.

1.

2.

3.

1. Stand with one shoulder next to a wall and your foot three inches from the wall. You may keep your arm straight or bent at the elbow.

   Without moving your body, try to push the wall away by using your upper arm. Push and hold that muscle tight for six to ten seconds.

2. Stand with your back against the wall and your heels three inches out from the wall. You may keep your arm straight or bent at the elbow.

   Without moving your body, push the back of your right upper arm against the wall. Push and hold that tightened muscle for six to ten seconds and relax.

3. Stand in a doorway and set one foot slightly ahead of the other to steady yourself. Stand so that the front of one shoulder and arm is "caught" on the door jamb. Keep that arm straight by your side, push forward against the door jamb, and hold the tightened muscle for six to ten seconds. Then relax (feel your upper arm and shoulders tighten).

B. ARMS

Do each exercise first with your left arm and then with your right arm.

Exercise Hints

- *These exercises are to strengthen your upper arm muscles.*
- *Concentrate and feel the muscles contract. As you pull up on the table the muscle on the front of your upper arm tightens. As you push down on the table, the muscle at the back of your arm tightens.*
- *If your shoulder or elbow is very sore, you will first have to find your "comfort-position" before you can tighten the muscles.*
- *A small towel between the table and your arm will provide a little padding.*

Lifestyle Tips

- If your hands are sore, you may find it helpful to put strap loop handles on things such as the oven door or drawers, etc. Then you can use your forearm to pull them open.
- A non-slip pad on your kitchen counter or work bench will reduce the stress required to stabilize an item.
- Loops of ribbon as handles on your bedclothes will help with adjusting your blankets.

1.

2.

1. Sit down in front of a heavy table. Place the palms of your hands under the table (or just above the wrists on your forearms with your thumbs up). Push up against the table with your palms. Hold the muscles tight for ten seconds, then relax.

2. Sit down in front of a heavy table. Place the palms of your hands on top of the table or, with your thumbs toward the ceiling, rest your forearms (just below the wrists) on the table. Push down on the table with your palms. Push and hold the muscles tight for ten seconds, then relax.

STRENGTHENING

LOWER BODY

- HIP
- KNEE
- ANKLE

II. LOWER BODY - Legs (Hip, knee and ankle joints)

Again refer to the joint category 1, 2, 3, 4, or 5 which you selected for each joint and repeat the following lower body strengthening exercises as indicated below. That is, if your hip is category 3, then repeat each hip exercise 20-30 times.

Category	Ellert-Parker Joint Classification System©	Repeat Exercise
1	Normal healthy joint, never been affected	30 times
2	A joint, at one time affected by arthritis, but today is cool and neither swollen nor painful	30 times
3	A joint that is a little swollen, neither hot nor painful	20 - 30 times
4	A joint that is swollen and hot or painful	at least 3 times and no more than 10 times
5	A joint which has been replaced (at present this category does not apply to the neck, wrist or back)	30 times

A. HIPS

Do each exercise first with your left leg and then your right leg.

Exercise Hints

- *With the first exercise, it is important to lift the leg about 10-12 inches off the bed, just high enough to make that leg muscle work without stressing your back. Tightening your tummy muscles will help support your back while your leg is in the air.*
- *With exercise two, the wider the belt the more comfortable it will feel. A small towel between the belt and your leg may be helpful.*
- *Exercise three is designed both for stretching and strengthening the hip area. You may be more comfortable if you allow your feet to hang over the end of the bed and if you place a small pillow under your tummy to stop you from arching your back.*
- *If you have low back pain you may wish to omit exercise three.*

Lifestyle Tips

- A long stick with double sided tape on the end of it is helpful when picking small things off the floor.
- Long-handled reachers are available; check with a medical supply store.
- A cane may be helpful until the muscles are strong enough to provide adequate support for the hip joint. The cane must be the correct length and held in the hand opposite to the sore limb.

1.

2.

3.

1. Lying on your side, tighten the muscles above the knee (quadriceps) of the leg closest to the ceiling.

   Lift the top leg up in the air toward the ceiling. Hold for six to ten seconds and return to starting position and relax.

2. Using a belt, loosely strap your legs together above your knees. Lie flat. Keep one leg still . . .

   and slide the other leg away from the still leg. Hold six to ten seconds and relax.

3. Lie on your stomach, keep your leg straight and tighten the muscle above your knee (quadriceps).

   Lift the leg into the air. Hold for six to ten seconds and relax.

B. KNEES

Do each exercise first with your left leg and then with your
right leg.

Exercise Hints

- *With both of these exercises set your hand on your thigh and you will be able to feel the quadriceps muscle tighten and work.*

Lifestyle Tips

- You may find it helpful to raise the height of the toilet seat.
- A bathtub grab bar and tub mat will help you stabilize yourself as you move around in the tub.
- As with the hip, a cane may be helpful as long as it is the correct length and held in the opposite hand to the sore limb.

1. Sit in a straight backed, firm seated chair, which does not have any arms. Straighten your leg and concentrate on tightening the muscle above your knee (quadriceps). Hold for six to ten seconds and relax.

2. With your feet firmly on the ground and one of your legs directly in front of the chair leg, bend that leg back to the chair leg so that your heel touches the leg of the chair. Now push your heel against the chair leg for six to ten seconds and relax.

C. ANKLES

Do this exercise with both ankles at the same time.

Exercise Hints

- *Concentrate so that you are able to feel the muscle in the back of your lower leg (calf muscle) working.*

Lifestyle Hints

- When your ankles are sore or swollen, put your feet up.
- Make sure that your knees are supported as well, when your feet are up.
- Push a bed cradle or pillows to the end of the bed, between the sheets, so that the top sheet and blankets do not put any unnecessary weight on your ankles.

1.

1. Hold on to something for support. Now go up on your toes so that you lift your heels about two inches off the floor . . .

    then slowly put your heels back on to the floor.

TRUNK MUSCLES

III. TRUNK MUSCLES - (back and chest)

The trunk muscles include both tummy and back muscles. They provide support to your back and are essential for good posture. Strong tummy muscles will help you move from a lying to sitting position without pushing or pulling on painful upper limbs.

These exercises can also help improve your endurance. If you are able to repeat each exercise enough times to make you out of breath, your heart and lungs will get a workout as well.

Do these exercises as recommended, gradually increasing the number of repetitions. Remember, pain is your guide. If increased pain is still present two hours after exercising, decrease the number of times you repeat the exercise next time.

The categories for assessing your back are:

> I. pain free
> II. some discomfort
> III. painful

I.   Pain free

If your back is pain free, do all three exercises. Start by doing each exercise 5 times, gradually increasing to a maximum of 30 times. If you remain pain free, increase the number of repetitions by 5 times every three days. That is:

Day 1 - 5 times each
Day 4 - 10 times each
Day 7 - 15 times each
Day 10 - 20 times each
Day 13 - 25 times each
Day 15 - 30 times each (maximum)

II.   Some discomfort

If your back feels a little painful or uncomfortable, you can do all three exercises but do not repeat them as many times. Start by doing each exercise 5 times, gradually increasing to a maximum of 15 times.

Day 1 - 5 times each
Day 4 - 10 times each
Day 7 - 15 times each (maximum)

III. Painful

If your back is painful the only exercise you should do is Number 1, the "pelvic tilt". Start by doing the exercise 5 times and gradually increase to 15 times (if you cannot do even 5 pelvic tilts then you should contact your doctor).

Pelvic Tilt only

Day 1 - 5 times each
Day 4 - 10 times each
Day 7 - 15 times each (maximum)

Relax after each set of five.

Some activities involving the trunk:

- Everything you do involves the spine and trunk muscles. Therefore, be aware of the *posture* and *position* of your body at all times!

Exercise Hints

- *Do all exercises smoothly and with good muscle control. It is better to do five properly than ten poorly.*
- *Do not push yourself if your back is painful.*

Lifestyle Tips

Posture! Posture! Posture!

- Good posture means sitting or standing with your head up, shoulders back, your seat muscles and tummy muscles pulled in and firm.
- When lifting anything, be sure to bend your knees and keep the object as close to you as possible. If your knees are painful, it may be easier to go down on one knee before lifting.
- When resting, lie with your knees slightly bent. A pillow under your knees may feel more comfortable. This position can help you relax your lower back.

1.

1. Pelvic Tilting: Lie flat on your bed with knees slightly bent. Tighten your tummy muscles and push your lower back into the bed, tilting the pelvis backward as you tighten your buttocks. Hold for a count of five, then relax.

2.

3.

2. Lie on the bed or floor with knees bent and arms by your side. Now raise your head and shoulders about six inches off the bed and hold for a count of five, slowly lie back down and relax.

3. Lie flat on the bed, with knees bent. Keeping your knees together and both shoulders touching the bed, slowly lower both legs to the left to touch the bed, then bring them back to the center. Now slowly lower them to the right, touch the bed and bring them back to the center.

RELAXING EXERCISES
Enjoy them - you have earned them!

I. JAW

You have made it to the last group of exercises! Last but not least. Now relax and yawn - it is a terrific exercise for the jaw!

1. Hold your head straight. Slowly open your mouth as wide as you can without forcing your jaw. Then slowly close your mouth.

- *You can check if your range of motion is increasing or decreasing in this joint by using your fingers to measure how wide your mouth opens. Open your mouth as wide as you can and put your fingers in your mouth. Your fingers should be one on top of the other rather than side by side.*

Lifestyle Tips

- Jaw pain may be described as an earache.
- If your jaw is sore, try to eat soft foods and cut your food into small pieces.

II. DEEP BREATHING (rib cage)

Lie flat. Put your hands on your rib cage. Breathe in slowly for a count of three and feel your rib cage expand. Hold your breath for a moment. Then push all the air out of your lungs and feel the rib cage collapse. Then relax and repeat. Do this five times, then stop and rest for a minute. Now repeat another five times.

III. GENERAL RELAXATION

Lying flat, systematically tighten all your muscles. Start at your toes.

Curl your toes
Tighten your knees
Tighten your seat muscles
Tense your shoulders
Close your eyes tight

Hold for a count of five, then . . .

relax your face, shoulders, seat, knees and finally your toes.

If it feels good, you may wish to repeat this two or three times.

LEISURE

OTHER ACTIVITIES

Some people are concerned about participating in various leisure activities or coping with travel when they have a disability. This section provides some information and suggestions on how you might approach these two important areas.

I.   LEISURE ACTIVITIES

A person needs both a daily exercise program and leisure activities. The leisure activities encourage relaxation and social contacts. The daily exercise serves to maintain and increase your flexibility and strength.

Hopefully your daily exercise program will help you to increase your choice of leisure activities.

For some people, finding leisure activities that they can do and will enjoy may be a challenge. For example, if your favourite sports are tennis, water skiing and snow skiing and you have some degree of joint damage in your legs or arms, there are better activities in which to participate actively. But if you enjoy a sport and do not want to give it up completely, then simply adjust the way you take part. You can "coach" from the sidelines, join in on the beach party or meet with your friends after the ski lifts have shut down. Do not cut yourself out. You can continue to understand and enjoy the enthusiasm of others and their tales about the sport. It may not be your ideal way to participate, but it is better than no contact at all.

The only drawback with this type of participation in sports is that it does not provide the exercise that *you* need. So, while "coaching" from the sidelines, keep following your exercise program and if necessary look for new activities and hobbies.

Points to consider before participating in any leisure activities:

1. Be honest with yourself. Consider if any of your joints are swollen or painful. Avoid activities or at least decrease activities which will cause stress or strain on the sore joints unnecessarily.

2. Wear good shoes (i.e. golf shoes, walking shoes, hiking boots). Proper support for your feet is essential and will help you to keep your body in proper alignment.

3. Quick starts and stops, as well as constant twisting and turning, add a tremendous amount of stress to the lower body joints and back (e.g. racquet sports).

4. You may be able to modify the way you do an activity in order to reduce the stress on the specific joints so that you can still enjoy the sport.

5. Look over the lifestyle tips in the book and see if you can adapt them to your activity. Remember, if you behave yourself now, respect what your sore joints are telling you and prevent unnecessary joint damage, maybe next year you will be in better shape to resume your normal activities!

Below is a list of activities ranging from singing to hiking. This list is meant to give you some new ideas about things you might try. Before you attempt any one of them, remember to consider the points I have just mentioned. Also, you may wish to decrease your involvement in something else for a while. That is, if you are already walking every day and want to start swimming as well, then decrease your walking. Try walking four days a week and swimming three days a week.

Art Galleries
Billiards
Bird Watching
CB Radio/Ham Radio
Camping
Cards
Chess
Computers
Cross Country Skiing
Cycling
Dancing
Fishing
Flying
Gardening
Gliding
Golfing
Hiking
Hot Air Ballooning

Ice/Roller Skating
Knitting/Crocheting
Macramé
Musical Instruments
Night School
Painting
Ping Pong
Pottery
Reading
Racquet Sports
Snow Skiing
Stamp/Coin Collecting
Swimming
Theatre
Walking
Weaving
Woodwork

TRAVEL

II. TRAVEL

When you travel, remember that you know your own limitations but a stranger may not have even noticed them. If you need assistance, do not hesitate to ask for it! Most people in the tourist industry are very helpful. You are paying for a service and they would like to make your journey as pleasant as possible. Also, other passengers are very obliging and will lift a bag off a shelf or help you with your coat - if you ask. If someone asked you for assistance, would you not help if you could?

There are many agencies that can provide travel information to people with special needs. Although the focus is generally directed toward people in wheelchairs, it is likely that these hotel chains, airlines or tour companies will be receptive to accommodating others with special needs.

The following is a list of some sources of information when travelling with special needs:

1. Transportation in Canada
    A Guide for Travellers with Special Needs
    Prepared by : Transportation Development Centre
    Transport Canada December 1981
    1000 Sherbrook Street West
    P.O. Box 549, Place de l'aviation
    Montreal, Quebec, H3A 2R3

    Provides information (1981) on:

    i) services and travel guides to major Canadian Cities
    ii) brief Travel Tips for wheelchair travellers
    iii) some rules, regulations and special services for Canadian air, train, bus and ferry travel.

2. Travel Information Centre
    Moss Rehabilitation Hospital
    12th Street and Tabor Road
    Philadelphia, Pennsylvania 19141
    (215) 329-5715

    Provides information for handicapped travellers on accommodation, transportation and tourist attractions in the U.S., Canada and abroad.

3. The Itinerary
   137 Bayonne Street
   New Jersey, 07002.

   A publication dealing with various topics of interest to disabled travellers.

4. The Hub, Physically Handicapped Service Center
   P.O. Box 4397
   St. John's, Nfld A1C 6C4

5. A Guide for the Disabled Traveller . . .
   The United States, Canada and Europe.
   by Frances Barish
   Frommer/Pasmantier Publications
   New York. 1984.

6. Access To The World: A Travel Guide
   For The Handicapped
   by Louise Weiss,
   Facts on File
   New York 1983

7. The United States Welcomes Handicapped Visitors:
   Society for the Advancement of Travel for the
      Handicapped
   Suite 803,
   1012 14th Street, N.W.
   Washington, D.C. 20005.

8. Travel agencies

   A few travel agencies specialize in travel for the handicapped. Ask the agent, before you make any arrangements, if the agency is familiar with ways of travelling for your special needs.

9. Contact your local public health unit for information about shots that may be required or potential health problems in other countries (e.g. water or climate).

10. Contact your local librarian to see if they have the above information or other sources of information.

Points to consider when travelling:

1. If you are concerned about travelling and making your own arrangements, you may wish to travel with an organized tour group. They generally make all your transportation and hotel arrangements, and ensure your baggage is taken from one station to the next.

2. When you book your ticket be sure to let the agent know what your needs are (e.g. a seat near the washroom, a wheelchair, etc.)

3. Be sure that you have enough travel insurance to cover any reasonable mishap that may occur (e.g. lost medication, hospitalization).

4. Carry all medication with you. Do not put it in your suitcase in case your luggage goes astray. Ask your doctor for the following information about your medication and then carry the information with you:
   i) what is the generic (international) name for my medication?
   ii) what dosage do I take?
   iii) what are my normal blood levels?
   iv) is there any other medical information I should carry with me?
   v) should I wear a medical alert bracelet?

5. Take along your splints and aids, such as dressing sticks or tap turners. If you are staying in a hotel or motel, you can leave a note for the maid regarding certain items (e.g. ask that they do not turn the taps off too tightly and explain why).

6. Use lightweight luggage with wheels. Take two small suitcases instead of one large one.

7. Carry-on baggage should have a shoulder strap and, if possible, wheels. If your hands are sore, you will have another way to carry the bag.

8. On long trips where they are sitting still for a long time (car, air, train or bus), many people will tend to stiffen up, whether or not they have arthritis. Every half hour, exercise your ankles and toes and then, once every hour, do as many of the stretching exercises as possible. If you are travelling by car, stop every hour and walk around for about five minutes. As you walk you can do your exercises. Lower body exercises can be done in the car.

9. Do not be too proud to ask an attendant for help if it would make things easier for you. You should save your energy for things that matter and times when no assistance is available.

10. Ask for a wheelchair to transport you through the terminal. Attendants do not question why you want one - but do give them notice of your requirements. Again, save your energy for more important and enjoyable things.

BOOKLIST

Most of these are pamphlets, but some are small books. Those from the Arthritis Society, unless otherwise indicated, are free. Those from the Arthritis Foundation are generally $0.10 a copy.

The Arthritis Society
250 Bloor Street East
Toronto, Ontario, Canada M4W 3P2

You, Your Child and Arthritis $2.00
Aids and Adaptations.. $2.55
Easy is The Name of the Game $1.00
Basic Facts About Arthritis $0.70

*   *   *

The Arthritis Society: B.C. and Yukon Division
895 West 10th Avenue
Vancouver, B.C. Canada V5Z 1L7

Lupus and You: A Guide for Patients $3.00
Your Hands — The Art of Self-Defence $1.50
Owner's Manual: Your Knee Replacement $1.25
Owner's Manual: Total Hip Replacement $1.00
Note: Please add 10% for postage and handling. Payment must be enclosed with order.

*   *   *

The Arthritis Foundation
1314 Spring Street, N.W.
Atlanta, Georgia, U.S.A. 30309

Systemic Lupus Erythematosus
Ankylosing Spondylitis
Psoriatic Arthritis
Polymyositis
Polymalgia Rheumatica
Bursitis, Tendinitis and Other Related Conditions
Quackery
Diet and Nutrition
Living and Loving
U.S. pamphlets are now available from The Arthritis Society in Ontario at a cost of $0.20 each.

*   *   *

* Facts About Gout
* Facts About Inflammation
* Facts About Osteoarthritis
* Facts About Rheumatoid Arthritis

* These pamphlets are generally available from your family doctor.
Prices are subject to change without notice.
Delivery — 4 to 6 weeks.